Coloring Affirmations

An empowering self-nourishing coloring book for positive change

~ Edward Felix Torres Charfauros ~

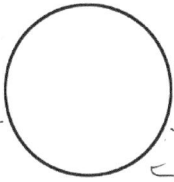

Coloring

Affirmations

An empowering self nourishing
coloring book for positive change

Edward.F.T.Charfauros@gmail.com   *https://EdwardFTCharfauros.com*

Coloring Affirmations
An empowering self-nourishing coloring book for positive change

"I am feasting upon the negative opinions and gobbling down the negative labels fueling my motivation! I am enjoying the positive support and sharing all the good stuff everywhere in between! I am inspiring my soul however I can and amusing my aspiration whenever I can while my success continues!"

Coloring Affirmations
An empowering self-nourishing coloring book for positive change

My doodle page

"I am imagining for myself the kind of outcomes that positively affect my life. I am creating opportunities for myself that positively affect my circumstances. I am motivated to continue my success doing what I am passionate about, enjoy doing, and love sharing."

Coloring Affirmations
An empowering self nourishing coloring book for positive change

My doodle page

"I can come up with better thoughts for better results, so I am thinking like so. I can talk better for better relationships, so I am talking like so. I can come up with better opinions for a better perspective, so I am proceeding like so. I am better than the negative labels given to me, so I am succeeding like so for my success to continue."

My doodle page

"I am dreaming brilliantly of my ideas
regarding what impassions me. I am
thinking intelligently about my
plans to take action. I am talking
positively about my intentions. I am
working smartly with my progress
for my ideal outcomes. I am loving
the success and everyone involved
because I am happily continuing my
life."

My doodle page

"I get out of bed to do what is necessary for my happiness toward sleeping satisfied. I get out of bed for excitement, for adventure, and for amusement. I get out of bed to do what I love, be around who I love, and go where I love to continue my greater life."

Coloring Affirmations
An empowering self-nourishing coloring book for positive change

My doodle page

"I am striving to be the kind of friend I desire to be around. I am striving to be the kind of success I desire to be about. I am choosing to be much more friendly and much more kind for the benefit of my future. I continue appreciating the loving friendships I encounter, and the success I create along my way."

Coloring Affirmations
An empowering self-nourishing coloring book for positive change

My doodle page

"I am acting the success I was born as! I am being the success I am meant to be! I am loving the success I am blessed as, being, and having! I am enjoying this life I am successfully born with, while I continue sharing it along throughout my way."

My doodle page

"I am making the best of my moments, situations and circumstances serve me. I am making the best of my opportunities, solutions, and ideas serve me. I am making the best of my relationships, interactions and communication serve me."

My doodle page

"I am going, I am continuing, and I am succeeding regardless of opinion. I am finishing, I am accomplishing, and I am still succeeding regardless of judgment. I am achieving, I am satisfying, and I am continuing to succeed regardless of who is involved."

Coloring Affirmations
An empowering self-nourishing coloring book for positive change

My doodle page

"I am proud of the progress and success I've made this far, and I am positively looking forward to continuing. I am proud of how far I've come, and I am positively looking forward to succeeding further. I am proud of what I've accomplished and achieved, and I am looking forward to more."

Coloring Affirmations
An empowering self-nourishing coloring book for positive change

My doodle page

I am striving toward improving myself with healthier choices, healthier decisions, and healthier thoughts that positively affect me physically and mentally. I am striving toward improving my life with healthier communication, healthier behavior, and a healthier attitude. I am striving toward improving my life with healthier interactions, healthier relationships, and healthier self management.

My doodle page

"I am going for my satisfaction and I am amusing myself. I am going for my pleasure and I am satisfying myself. I am going for my bliss and I am pleasing myself. I am going for my amusement and I am enjoying myself."

Coloring Affirmations
An empowering self nourishing coloring book for positive change

My doodle page

I am unafraid of achieving my dreams and accomplishing my goals. I am thankful for the progress and success I am achieving for the desirable outcomes I want to realize. I am grateful now, and I continue looking forward with excitement for a more prosperous future to benefit from.

My doodle page

"I am the kind of winner who appreciates learning from losses while learning to improve for better. I am the kind of winner who achieves progress and succeeds in accomplishing milestones, goals and satisfying results. I am continuing as the success that I am toward continuing an awesome life."

My doodle page

"I am beginning anew here and now with positive thoughts for positive results. I am choosing positive affecting affirmations supporting results that I perceive to be beneficial. I am encouraging positive affecting emotions that support my continued path of success and adventurous life journey."

Coloring Affirmations
An empowering self-nourishing coloring book for positive change

My doodle page

"I love myself enough to keep myself out of trouble while focusing upon all that pleases me. I love myself enough to focus upon the good stuff of life while enjoying myself throughout my day. I love myself enough to keep going while focusing upon success."

My doodle page

"I am positively thinking and focusing on better situations and circumstances for my life. I am confidently believing and focusing on bettering my attitude and behavior for myself. I am happily choosing and focusing on better outcomes and results for my future."

Coloring Affirmations
An empowering self-nourishing coloring book for positive change

My doodle page

Coloring Affirmations
An empowering self nourishing coloring book for positive change

I am leading myself toward becoming much more than what I already am and desire to be. I am leading myself toward all that I desire to do with my life, my day, and my self. I am leading myself into a much more satisfying and wonderful future.

My doodle page

"I am taking control of my dreams and progressing with optimism and enthusiasm toward my accomplishments and achievements. I am appreciative of my progress throughout my journey of success while I look forward to a positive difference in my life. I am positively sharing my success, progress, and experiences with others along my way for positive affecting changes.

Coloring Affirmations
An empowering self nourishing coloring book for positive change

My doodle page

"I am making it a goal to enjoy myself wherever I attend regardless of who I am with. I am making it a goal to enjoy myself with whatever I am doing regardless of what it is. I am making it a goal to enjoy myself with whoever I am with regardless of who it may be. The better I am, the better it can be!"

Coloring Affirmations

An empowering self nourishing coloring book for positive change

My doodle page

"I am thankful for the power to positively affect my life, my success, and my future how I deserve it to be. I am thankful for the power to be determined, to be motivated, and to be positive as my success continues. I am thankful for the power of love, the power of change, and the power of thought."

Coloring Affirmations
An empowering self nourishing coloring book for positive change

My doodle page

Coloring Affirmations
An empowering self nourishing coloring book for positive change

I continue sharing where I can, when I can, how I can, and with whom I can, with what have. I continue assisting others where I can, when I can, and how I can wherever I am with whatever I have. I continue doing it all, attending wherever, enjoying myself with whomever, and purposely endeavoring however with some level of love.

My doodle page

Coloring Affirmations
An empowering self nourishing coloring book for positive change

I appreciate the challenges that strengthen my will, strengthen my mind, and strengthen my character. I appreciate the lessons that help me improve my life, improve my career, and improve my self. I appreciate the difficulties that assist me with my education, assists me with my experiences, and assists me with my satisfaction.

My doodle page

"I have no better choice than to love who I am and appreciate who I was while I enthusiastically look forward to who I am becoming. I have no better choice than to focus on the present moment for my life, my future, and my success everywhere throughout my life with great optimism. I have no better choice than to make the best of what I have, as I happily look forward to what I am going to have."

Coloring Affirmations
An empowering self nourishing coloring book for positive change

My doodle page

"I am not allowing others to negatively affect my thoughts for anything worse. I am not allowing others to negatively affect my situation and circumstances. I am not allowing myself to worsen my life, my present moment and my future. I am separating myself from the negative influences to continue successfully."

My doodle page

"I am continuing to make the best use of my situations serve me while I continue taking advantage of opportunities to benefit me. I am continuing optimistically while I convert all the negativity I create into motivational fuel to better my circumstances and excite my future. I am my greatest challenge and I am my greatest resolution to continue my success!"

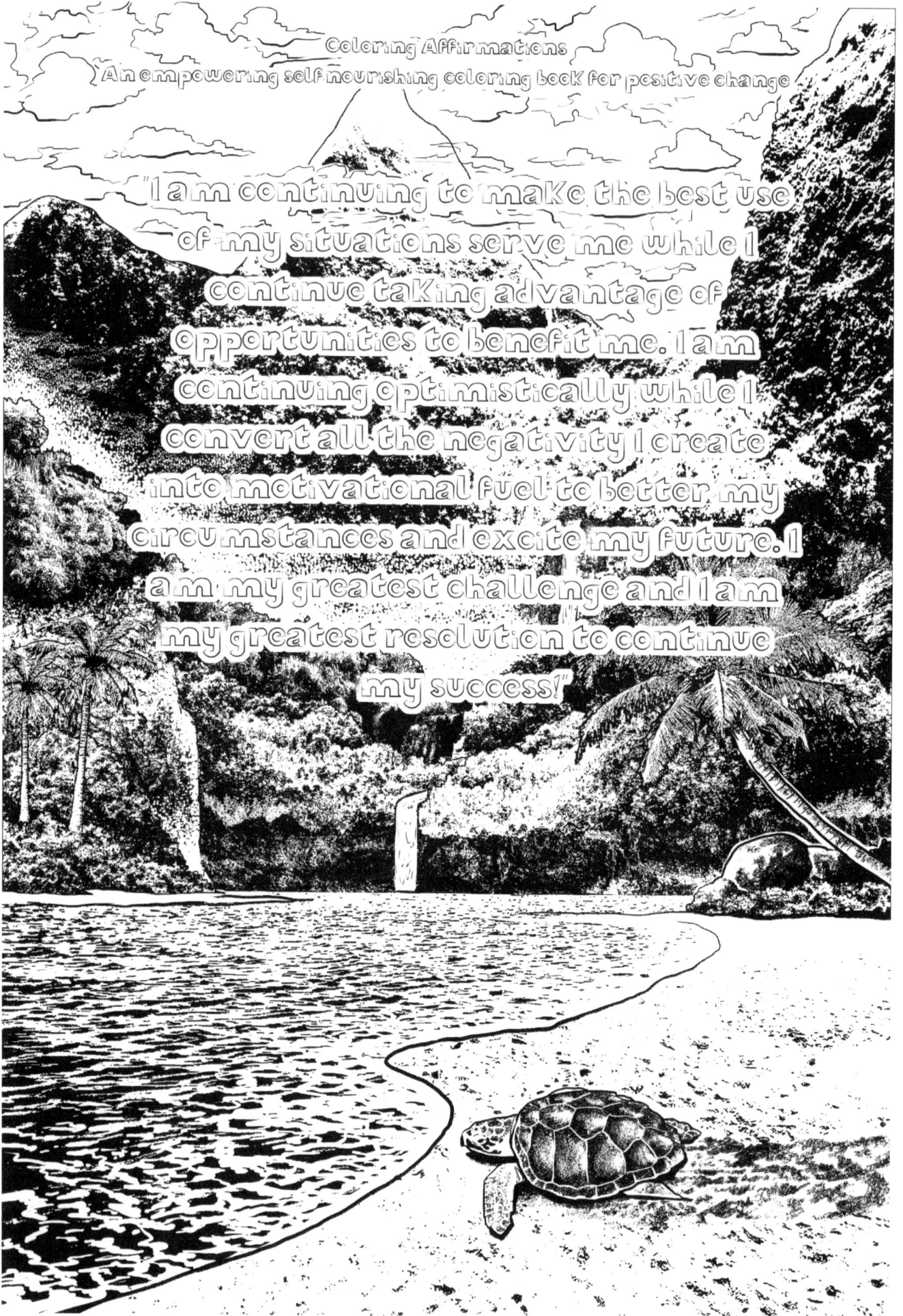

My doodle page

I continue supporting my strengths and encouraging my genius doing what I love with purpose. I continue sharing my passions, serving with purpose, and appreciating the support throughout my progress and success. I continue humbly toward all my achievements and accomplishments while enjoying myself along my way."

Coloring Affirmations
An empowering self-nourishing coloring book for positive change

My doodle page

Coloring Affirmations
An empowering self nourishing coloring book for positive change

"I am nourishing my mind with positive thoughts toward positive results. I am nourishing my thoughts with positive ideas for positive changes. I am nourishing my changes with positive affecting good vibes, good communication, good attitude, and good behavior.

My doodle page

"I am fueling my passions and motivating my purpose by taking the negative affecting criticisms, ugly labels, and horrible opinions to strengthen my will and desires. I am converting negativity into various forms of benefits for my continued success. I am continuing my success in some form or manner one way or another from this day to the next this moment forward."

Coloring Affirmations
An empowering self nourishing coloring book for positive change

My doodle page

Coloring Affirmations
An empowering self nourishing coloring book for positive change

"I am succeeding forward optimistically with an attitude of gratitude and with action for positive results. I am succeeding forward by actively making progress through my positive thinking, goal setting, active planning, thoughtful preparation, and decisive action. I am succeeding forward with better thoughts, better behavior, better communication, better attitude, and better interaction to continue my success.

Coloring Affirmations
An empowering self nourishing coloring book for positive change

My doodle page

www.ingramcontent.com/pod-product-compliance
Lightning Source LLC
LaVergne TN
LVHW072124070426
835511LV00003B/83